Maypoles and Wood Demons

THE MEANING OF TREES

Maypoles
and
Wood
Demons

THE MEANING OF TREES

BY ELIZABETH S. HELFMAN
drawings by Richard Cuffari

THE SEABURY PRESS · NEW YORK

SPECIAL THANKS to Mrs. Hattie Carthan,
who provided information about a magnolia tree in Brooklyn,
and to my perceptive and helpful editors,
James Giblin and Laura Kassos.

*for
Ruth*

Contents

CHAPTER 1   *Imagine a World Without Trees*   9

CHAPTER 2   *People of the Forest*   17

CHAPTER 3   *A Tree Named Yggdrasil*   25

CHAPTER 4   *Other World Trees*   33

CHAPTER 5   *Trees of Life*   41

CHAPTER 6   *Sacred Trees*   53

CHAPTER 7   *Demons, Dryads, and Fairies*   65

CHAPTER 8   *Trees for Luck and Celebration*   77

CHAPTER 9   *Gifts from Trees*   91

CHAPTER 10   *Plant a Tree*   105

CHAPTER 11   *Save a Tree*   117

BOOKS FOR FURTHER READING   *123*

INDEX   *125*

CHAPTER

1

*Imagine
a
World
Without
Trees*

IMAGINE a world without trees. No grove of trees in a city park where children can play in the shade. No green boughs of pine and spruce to catch the first snowfall of winter. No pattern of leafless branches against the cold, still sky. No miracle of new leaves in the springtime.

There would be no whisper of summer wind along the boughs as you walk in a park. You would never hear, in autumn, the rustle of dry leaves around your feet, telling you that winter is on its way, spring will follow, and the whole cycle of new growth will begin again for every living thing.

Trees are the largest plants in the world. Their strong woody trunks hold them upright and branches grow from the trunks. Smaller branches grow from large ones; twigs are the smallest. Green leaves grow on the branches.

Many trees lose all of their leaves in the fall. Leaf buds

cling to the branches through the winter and uncurl into new leaves when spring comes. Evergreens lose their leaves, too, but not all at once. They remain green throughout the winter. The leaves of pines and some other evergreens are called needles; that is what they look like.

Most people see only the part of a tree that is above ground. There is just as much of it underground—numerous branching roots, big and little, that have grown deep into the earth. The length of these roots, taken all together, would add up to many miles.

A tree grows by one of the most ingenious processes in all the natural world. Thousands of tiny growing tips on the ends of the roots take in water from the soil, along with nitrogen, potash, phosphorus, and various other elements the tree needs for its growth. This mixture is the sap of the tree. The sap travels up the trunk in tiny tubes clustered around the heartwood at its center. Through these tubes it reaches every branch and every leaf.

The leaves are the food-making part of the tree. In the sunlight they take in a gas called carbon dioxide from the air and combine it with the water in the sap to make the sugars that are food for the tree. This food then travels down the trunk of the tree in other tiny tubes that circle the trunk just inside the bark. It helps build every part of the tree that grows.

It takes tremendous amounts of water to accomplish all

this. Yet only a small part of the water that travels up the trunk is actually used in making food for the tree. All the rest is evaporated from the leaves into the air.

The leaves do something else while they are making food for the tree. They give off oxygen. This is important for people. Every person in the world, and every animal, must breathe in oxygen to stay alive. Our bodies use the oxygen in the air. Then we breathe out carbon dioxide, which helps leaves make food for all the green plants in the world.

The amount of oxygen given off by the leaves of trees is tremendous. An acre of young trees can produce enough oxygen in a year to keep eighteen people alive. The trees in city parks and along city streets help dilute the polluted air by making oxygen.

That is not all trees do for us. We are grateful for their cool shade on a hot day. They slow down strong winds that might batter us and our houses. In cities and along busy highways trees absorb sound and make the world around them seem much less harsh and noisy.

Many trees provide food and shelter for birds and other creatures. They can be a shelter for you in the rain, for people on camping trips, for children who build tree houses. The strong branch of a tree may be the best place to hang a swing to carry you up in the air and down again.

Tree leaves fall to the ground, decay there, and help make rich soil. Tree roots hold rain water in the earth so it does not

all run off the land, into streams and away. There are many other practical uses for trees; a later chapter in this book tells about some of them.

There is a grove of trees on a little hill in a New York City park—three maples, a birch, and two oaks. Children often play under the trees. They scuff the fallen leaves in the autumn and look with wonder as new green leaves uncurl on the branches in the spring. On hot summer days families come carrying lunches in brown paper bags and sit happily in the shade of the trees.

The largest tree in the grove is an oak, a trim, straight tree with many branches. The lower ones turn down toward the ground, invitingly. This oak was a young tree on the hill before any of the people who sit in its shade were born. Year after year it has lived and grown in the sun.

Year after year the children have come, and the families with brown paper bags. Children have grown up, and many have gone away. Some have forgotten the trees in the park. Others will never forget. For them the little grove was a special place, with a hint of magic about it. They remember feeling at peace with all the world as they sat under the trees, in the shade that was dappled with sunlight. Wind in the leaves seemed to whisper to them, saying that all was well in the world as long as trees grew from the earth and reached for the sun.

Other people, in earlier times, have felt that there was something very special about trees. Some have believed that the first people in the world came from trees. Many were certain that the world itself was held in place by an enormous tree. There was a great magic in trees, they said. This book is about some of this magic and the wonderfully varied meaning of trees to people.

CHAPTER
2

*People
of
the
Forest*

THE FIRST people on earth lived in the gloom and quietness of endless forests. We are not sure just when this was; the earliest probably lived more than two million years ago. Almost the whole world of these early people was trees. There were countless tree trunks all around them, and up above, a green roof of leafy branches all but hid the sky.

The trees of that time were much like those that grow on earth today. These trees and their ancestors had survived through millions of years during which there were violent changes in the climate of the earth. They survived the Ice Age a million years ago when huge glaciers gradually moved south over large areas of North America and Europe. Whole forests were hurled down and buried in ice then, but the seeds of trees were pushed southward with the ice. Wherever it was warm enough the seeds sprouted and grew more trees. When the ice retreated, seeds moved north, blown on the wind or carried by birds. In time the earth that had been scraped and denuded by the glaciers was covered with forests again.

People, too, survived the Ice Age. These were hardy people, but they were not equipped to live in cold places. They moved south to escape the ice and then north again in the warmer periods that followed.

We do not know how the earliest people felt about their forest home. Their lives must have been full of danger and uncertainty. Fierce animals roamed the woods—animals that hunted people, as people hunted them. Hunger could be the worst enemy of all. And yet these people must have known that their very lives depended on this world of trees. The forest provided them with food and sheltered them from the rain and the sun. It was the forest that gave people whatever peace and comfort they knew.

Perhaps we can understand a little of how early people felt about their forest by finding out about people who live in the forest today. There are not many, but here and there in different parts of the world small groups of people live much as the earliest people lived. They hunt animals for food; they fish; they gather edible plants, fruits, and roots that grow in the forest.

The BaMbuti Pygmies live in the tropical Ituri Forest, almost exactly in the middle of Africa. Their forest is warm all year round. Gigantic trees drip with the water of frequent

rainstorms. To us this forest might seem like a place of damp, depressing gloom, too silent and too lonely to endure. But that is not how it seems to the Pygmies. To them it is a shady world in which the dense treetops let just enough sunlight filter through. It is cool and restful, unlike the world outside where the hot sun dries up the earth.

The forest does not seem to the Pygmies a silent place. It is full of exciting sounds, all of which have meaning for them. There are a multitude of small animal sounds among the trees, the joyful singing of brightly colored birds, and the voices of the people themselves. This is not, to them, a lonely place.

The Pygmies call themselves "Children of the Forest." They have lived there for thousands of years, and the forest

has never failed to supply them with all their needs. Their shelters are built with saplings and covered with large leaves. The little clothing they wear is made from sheets of bark, pounded with a mallet made from an elephant tusk. There is no need to store food or raise crops. Fruits, nuts, and game are always close at hand.

These are gentle people who live in harmony with their environment. The forest to them is a wonderful world, and they sing a chorus in praise of it. The sound of their singing echoes among the tall trees. "The forest is good," they sing, "the forest is kind. The forest gives us all."

It has been many years since most people lived in forests. About ten thousand years ago some of the early people learned to grow their own grain. They cleared away trees and brush to make open spaces where they could plant their gardens. People moved out of the forest and settled in villages beside their fields. They could grow more food in these fields than they had been able to gather when they lived in the forest.

Grain could be stored at harvest time and eaten in winter. People no longer had to live only in the warm places of the earth. They made houses for shelter and simple clothing of bark and leaves. Life was easier than it had ever been before.

The vast forest no longer seemed to these people a safe and sheltering place. Instead it became a mysterious region where unknown dangers lurked. Terrible beasts, some real and some imagined, roamed the forests. Wild men and out-laws hid there. Strange cries could be heard echoing on the wind. Tales and legends from these times tell of the terrors of the unknown woods that were no longer home to most of mankind.

But though the forest seemed a frightening place, few people would have wanted a world without any trees at all. A grove of trees was one of the loveliest things on earth, and in those times, as now, there was nothing more comforting than the shade of a tree on a hot summer day.

Early people saw flowers, trees, and other plants change with the seasons. In the fall most things that grew from the earth seemed to die. Only the evergreens looked alive. Winter might be long and very cold, but when spring came all the world was alive again. Tender pink leaves unfolded from buds and changed to green. Blossoms appeared, some big and colorful, some small and inconspicuous. Then came the fruits, nuts, and seeds that were food for mankind.

It seemed to early people that spirits and gods inhabited their world and created the wonders found in it. People wor-shiped these spirits and the gods. Gifts were offered to them —often animals killed in the hunt and the fruits of the earth. Ceremonies were invented to please the gods.

Surely, people thought, there were spirits in trees. They dreamed of trees and worshiped trees, danced around them and peopled the wild forests with creatures of their imagination. Through thousands of years a fabulous folklore of trees grew up as people tried to understand their own feelings about the leafy world around them.

CHAPTER

3

A
Tree
Named
Yggdrasil

THERE WAS much that early people did not understand about the world. They wondered why the bright sun in the sky did not fall to earth. They asked what kept the moon and the stars in the night sky. Since the sun and the moon and the stars did not fall, something must be holding up the sky itself.

Many people who lived in mountainous countries believed that a huge mountain held up the sky. People who lived on plains thought that it was held up by a world tree with a big trunk and spreading branches. Still other people believed in a world tree on top of a world mountain. These early people thought that the earth was a circular disk. No one at that time knew that the world is a sphere.

People in many different parts of the world believed in a world tree. Most of them did not learn this from other peoples; each group of people thought up their own world tree. The earliest one we know much about was invented by people who lived almost six thousand years ago, in the valley of the Tigris and Euphrates rivers in Asia Minor. The roots of this tree, they believed, extended into the depths below the earth. From these depths came springs of fresh water that made the rivers of the world. The branches of this tree had held up the sky even before there were people. They spread over all the world. The leaves of the tree were clouds, and they cast great shadows on the earth. The tree's fruit was the stars.

The world trees of other people often resembled this earliest one. But there were differences, too, and it is these differences that fascinate us.

Scandinavian people of northern Europe told tales of their own world tree. They said it was the greatest and best of all. This tree was an ash named Yggdrasil. Its mighty trunk pierced the flat disk of the world. Its branches held up the sky, the stars, and the clouds.

Yggdrasil was forever green, though four stags browsed ceaselessly on its foliage. (Each stag represented one of the four great winds.) The dew that fell from the tree onto the earth was called honey-dew, and it was the food of bees.

Yggdrasil had three great roots. One grew down into a place of mist and darkness below the earth. This was the world of the dead. Another root grew into the cold and cheerless land of giants who were covered with frost and

27

ice. The third grew upward into Asgard, the high mountain that was the home of the gods. Below this third root was the well of Urd where the gods met every day to settle disputes and discuss problems.

Three Norns, or Fates, lived beside the well of Urd. They guarded the tree and watered it every day with sacred water from the fountain. This kept the tree green and strong. The three Norns represented the past, the present, and the future. They controlled the lives of all people.

Yggdrasil was constantly threatened by living creatures that preyed upon it. There were always the four stags. On the highest bough sat an eagle with a hawk perched between his eyes. This eagle symbolized the air and knew many things.

The hawk could see far into the distance; he was a lookout for the gods.

At the root that grew in the world of the dead lived a great serpent named Nidhögg, along with smaller snakes. They gnawed forever at the roots of the tree, wanting to destroy it. The serpent was at war with the eagle that sat on the topmost branch. A nimble squirrel named Ratatösk, bent on trouble, ran up and down the tree carrying messages of hate from one to the other. He would tell the serpent that the eagle intended to tear him to pieces. Then he would go back to the top of the tree and tell the eagle that the serpent was planning to devour him. This squirrel was said to represent rain and snow.

Beneath the root of the tree in the land of the frost-giants was the well of the giant Mimir the wise. Whoever drank of this well would know beforehand everything that would ever happen.

There are many stories about the ash Yggdrasil. One tells of the time when Odin, leader of the gods, sacrificed himself to himself. He pierced himself with a spear and hung suffering on the great tree, shaken by the wind, for nine days and nights. Odin himself says, in the old verse:

> *I know that I hung on the windy tree*
> *For nine whole nights,*
> *Wounded with the spear, dedicated to Odin,*

Myself to myself,
On that tree
Of which no one knows
From what root it springs.

Odin was performing a magic rite on the tree. The gods, like people, grew old. Magic could make them strong and young again.

While he hung on the tree Odin saw beneath him some runes, magic signs carved in stone. He made a mighty effort that caused him to groan with pain, bent down, and lifted up the runes. Their magic power set him free. He dropped to the ground and found that he was wiser than ever before and capable of doing great deeds. Because he had sacrificed himself on the windy tree, Odin could start life over again.

The gods who lived in Asgard fought many wars against demons and giants in its defense. Whenever this happened the tree Yggdrasil trembled to its very roots. The old stories tell about the most terrible conflict of all. The gods fought giants and frightful monsters that had been let loose. Odin himself was swallowed by a wolf of incredible size. This time none of the gods survived. The human race was swept from the surface of the earth. Stars fell from the sky, and all the earth was on fire. Then the seas rose and covered all things.

But life began again. A new green world was born from the wreckage of the old. There were new gods. The ash

31

Yggdrasil had not been destroyed in the flames. Inside it a man and a woman had hidden all through the destruction of the world, fed only with morning dew. The Scandinavians said that all the people who live upon the earth came from this man and woman and their children. The ash Yggdrasil, though its very roots trembled in the great conflict, had saved the human race.

CHAPTER
4

Other World Trees

To the people of Scandinavia the ash Yggdrasil was the most wonderful tree in the world. Indeed, the world could not have existed without it. Other people, in other places, had their own ideas of a world tree just as wonderful to them.

In India a world tree was known by different names at different times. Under the name of Kalpadruma it was a colossal cloud tree growing on a steep mountain. Before the sun and the moon were created, the shadow of this tree made day and night. Bright flowers and singing streams of clear water surrounded it. Those who approached it gained wisdom and great happiness.

At other times this Hindu world tree was called Soma. From the branches of the Soma flowed a wonderful juice. Birds sat on the branches and pressed out the juice all day and all night. Whoever drank it would never die. The gods made the heavens and the earth from this tree, and from it came the seeds of all the flowers and fruits that grow on earth.

An ancient legend of the Buddhists in India tells about a gigantic tree growing from the center of the world. It was said that beneath this spot, in the watery depths where life begins, a serpent was coiled. It was he who supported the whole earth. A spring bubbled forever at the foot of the tree. A golden sunbird perched on its top.

Northeast of India, in the country called Tibet, the world tree was said to grow on a high mountain. It was called "far-spreading willow." Like other world trees, its roots were deep below the earth, in the realm of the dead. It grew up through the world of living people, and its top was in heaven with the gods.

This tree had six branches and on each branch sat a bird with a nest and an egg. Out of these eggs would come all the life in the world. On one branch sat a wild eagle with a turquoise-colored egg. Here, as in Scandinavia, the eagle was a bird of wisdom. We will find him sitting on other world trees.

In the Bible we read that a king named Nebuchadnezzar had a dream about a world tree. He told it to the Prophet Daniel:

> Thus were the visions of mine head in my bed;
> I saw, and behold a tree in the midst of the earth,
> and the height thereof was great.

35

The tree grew, and was strong, and the height thereof reached unto heaven, and the sight thereof to the end of all the earth:

The leaves thereof were fair, and the fruit thereof much, and in it was meat for all: the beasts of the field had shadow under it, and the fowls of the heaven dwelt in the boughs thereof, and all flesh was fed of it.

The world tree of the Chinese was a cassia. The leaves of this tree are always green and its bark smells like cinnamon. The cassia world tree was said to have been growing since time began. No one could even imagine how tall it was. It grew in paradise, far up in high mountains near Tibet, where the great Yellow River has its beginning. It was said that whoever entered paradise and ate of the fruit of this tree would be immortal.

The Japanese world tree was an enormous metal pine that grew in the north at the center of the world.

There were people in Central Asia who believed that a fierce dragon lived in the sea at the foot of Zambu, their world tree. Leaves dropped from the tree and the dragon caught as many as he could and ate them. Those he could not catch sank to the bottom of the sea and turned into gold.

In another Central Asian tale there was a serpent that wound itself around the world tree. An eagle lived on its top and pecked at its leaves. Sometimes the eagle flew furiously about, causing great storms.

Serpents (or dragons) and eagles remind us again of the great world tree Yggdrasil of the Scandinavians.

The Yakuts, people who live in northeastern Siberia, have a wonderful tale about their world tree. This tree was so old that its age could not be counted in centuries. Its roots grew far into the watery depths. Strange creatures dwelt there. (Serpents, perhaps.) The top of the tree rose over the seven stories of heaven. A heavenly yellowish liquid fell from its crown. When weary passersby drank this they were refreshed; the hungry were satisfied.

The bark and knots of this tree were silver, its sap was golden, and its leaves were as wide as the hide of a horse. These were talking leaves. When they rustled in the wind the tree conversed with the beings of the sky.

To this tree came the first man who ever walked on earth. He had been born at the center of the world, its navel. This, according to the Yakuts, is the quietest place on earth, where the moon does not wane, the sun does not set, and summer goes on forever while the cuckoo sings.

Some Yakut stories say this man was called "the Lonely Man," because he was alone on earth; there were no other human beings. He wanted to know what the world was like and why he was there. So he looked about him. In the East he saw the giant world tree growing out of a mighty hill in the middle of a broad plain. In the South he saw a quiet lake of milk in a grassy field. In the North he saw a dark forest where many animals lived, and behind the forest were high mountains with caps like white rabbit skin, leaning against the heavens. In the West he saw bushes, a forest of tall firs, and mountain peaks beyond the forest.

The Lonely Man knew where he should go. He walked across the wide plain to the world tree. The journey took many days and many nights. At last the great tree loomed before him. He spoke thus to the Spirit of the Tree: "Honored High Mistress, spirit of my tree, everything in the world lives in twos. They have offspring like themselves. Only I am alone. I wish a wife of my own kind; I wish to live as a man should. I ask this humbly with bowed head and bent knees."

The leaves of the tree began to murmur and a fine milk-white rain dripped from them upon the Lonely Man. The tree groaned, and from under its roots arose the Spirit of the Tree in the form of a woman with flowing hair. She offered the man milk to drink and blessed him, so that nothing could ever harm him—not water, or fire, or anything on earth. The Spirit of the Tree told the Lonely Man that his father was the heaven god Ar-tojon, and that soon after he was born his mother had lowered him from the third heaven to the earth, so that he could become the father of the human race.

The Lonely Man felt a hundred times stronger than he had before. He went away from the tree knowing that he would find a wife, and that he could do whatever must be done.

The Russians told about a world tree that was a mammoth oak growing on an island. Among its branches the sun disappeared each evening, to rest until dawn. Each morning the sun arose from the branches, refreshed. A dragon guarded the tree and the Maiden of the Dawn lived inside its trunk.

On the other side of the world, Indians called Aztecs, who lived in Mexico, made pictures of a world tree. They showed it standing, like so many others, in the center of the world. Its roots extended deep into the waters under the earth and its branches reached up to the clouds, as if in search of rain. The Aztecs worshiped this tree as Tota, "our Father."

Far away in New Zealand, the Maoris believed in a great father of forests named Tane-Mahuta. He was himself a colossal tree. He stood with his head on the earth while he held up the sky with his feet.

These are only a few of the tales of a world tree told in many parts of the world. Each tale grew out of the need for early people to explain the wonderful and mysterious world in which they lived.

CHAPTER

5

*Trees
of
Life*

THE WORLD tree was often called a tree of life. Many people believed that without this tree there would be no life on earth. It was needed by the realm of the dead, the world of living people, and the sky above the earth.

Other trees were said to bring life to the earth in different ways. Some people believed that the first human beings in the world came from trees. The Scandinavians have their story of the man and woman who hid in the Yggdrasil ash during the great upheaval of the world. They were the ancestors of all the people who came after.

There is another Scandinavian story that tells of the first people who ever lived on earth. It goes like this: The god Odin was walking one day by the seashore with his two brothers. Heaven and earth had been created, but there were as yet no people. The three brothers found two trees on the shore and decided to breathe life into them. Odin gave

42

each one a soul. One of his brothers gave them understanding, and the other gave each a face, speech, sight, and hearing. One tree was called Askr, the ash, and it became a man. The other was Embla, the elm, and it became a woman.

The ancient Greeks told of how Zeus, chief of all the Greek gods, created the first people from an ash. The Romans, on the other hand, said the first people came from an oak tree.

Among the ancient legends of Ireland was a story that the first man was created from an alder tree and the first woman from a mountain ash.

The Hereros who live in Southwest Africa believe that a very old tree they call Omumborombonga was the father of the people of their tribe and also of their cattle. The Hereros carry a bunch of green twigs when they pass this tree. They bow reverently. Then they put the green twigs on a branch or throw them on the ground at the foot of the tree as a kind of offering to their ancient ancestor. People converse with Omumborombonga. A man says something to the tree and then, in a changed voice, gives the answer the tree has whispered to him.

Along the west coast of Africa the iroko, or African Oak, is considered the source of human life. There is a story that tells how the first men and women climbed down to earth from the branches of an enormous mythical iroko tree.

The Ashanti, people of West Africa, hold special ceremonies in a sacred grove at the spot where they say the first

people came up out of the ground. People must take off their sandals and wear no hat when they enter this holy place. A sheep is sacrificed as a gift to the gods at a sacred fig tree in the grove.

The Ainu who live on the most northern islands of Japan believe that when God created the first man he made his backbone from the wood of a willow tree. The backbone, say the Ainu, is the most important part of a human being. His soul lives there. The willow is God's tree, and he gave a part of it to mankind.

In ancient Egypt many people believed that after a person died his soul had to go on a long journey to reach the Islands of the Blest, where he would be happy forever. First the soul must cross a vast and terrible desert. There a bird or an insect, such as a praying mantis, a grasshopper, or a butterfly, would be his guide. Soon the soul would come to a wonderful green tree growing in the desert. This was the sycamore fig, a tree that produces delicious fruit and also gives out a milklike fluid.

From this tree a goddess would emerge, or sometimes part of the goddess, perhaps just her arm. She would offer the traveler a dish of fruit or loaves of bread, and she would pour milk or water for him. (The milk of the tree was the milk of the goddess.) Once the soul had accepted these gifts, he became a guest of the goddess. He could not then return to the world of the living without her permission, but refreshed, he could continue on his long way to the Islands of the Blest.

The sycamore fig was a tree of life to the soul on its difficult journey. It was also said to provide nourishment for people on earth who worshiped the goddesses of this tree. Pictures on Egyptian monuments show a goddess of the sycamore fig bending over the earth, pouring water from the river Nile onto the fields of grain.

The Aztecs in Mexico thought of the universe as being divided into five regions. Four of these regions represented the four directions: east, north, west, and south. The fifth region was our own world. An Aztec painting shows these regions in a kind of diagram. At each of the four directions stands a cross-shaped tree of life. On the top of each tree sits a bird. At the center of the painting, in our own world, stands a god who was called the Heart of the Mountain.

The flowering tree of the red region of the East, at the top of the picture, rises up from a Temple of the Sun. On its top is perched, in glowing colors, the quetzal, sacred bird of Aztec priests and chiefs. Only they were allowed to wear its plumes.

The tree of the green North, at the right of the picture, rises from the jaws of earth itself. On its top sits a yellow parrot.

The West is blue in the picture. Its somewhat spiky tree

grows out of the body of a creature that may be a dragon. The bird on the top of the tree is a hummingbird. The Aztecs believed that the hummingbird died in the dry season and came to life again with the rainy season.

At the left of the picture, in the yellow-colored South, a curious split tree covered with thorns rises from a bowl. Its bird is a white eagle with bristling feathers. We have met this bird of wisdom on the top of other legendary trees.

Various gods are seen on each side of the four trees. Beside the tree of the North, for example, the god of life-giving maize faces his opposite, the Lord of the Dead.

Priests spent years studying the complicated Aztec system of beliefs. They expressed these beliefs in a symbolic kind of writing and in paintings. The Aztec people themselves had little learning; they did not fully understand the intricate designs their priests made.

Today we understand these designs even less, but it seems clear that the four trees in the Aztec scheme of the world represented the special character of the gods of each region. The Aztecs probably also believed that the four trees held up the heavens—that without them the sky would fall down and there could be no life on earth.

The Aztecs believed that a life-giving tree also grew in the world of the dead. This tree is shown in an early painting. Its fruits are the souls of infants, warmly wrapped. These infants did not live long enough on earth to know joy or sor-

47

row, so they will be born again. Milk drips from the tree to nourish them while they wait to see the light of the sun.

The cedar, an evergreen, is a sacred tree of life to the Arikara Indians who live on the North American prairie. They call it "Grandmother of life." The evergreens, they say, make all the world green.

Like other evergreens, the cedar stays green all year long. It tells the Indians that life will continue year after year, just as its foliage continues. Yet much of the world seems to die each winter and come alive again in the spring. People feel this in themselves; it is as if they were born again each spring. Because life must be renewed each year, the Arikara Indians annually perform the ceremony of the sacred cedar.

Every summer they hold a festival that lasts four days. The second day is a celebration of the sacred Grandmother Cedar. A fine cedar is cut down and brought to the camp. There the people greet it joyfully and smother it with gifts —yards of colored cloth, bright feathers, peeled willow branches symbolizing horses.

All the people are very gay. They play games and sing and dance for hours. The tree is then carried into the Indians' great lodge, and there is a ceremony in which a fan of hawk feathers is fastened to its top. This cedar is now different from all others; it is sacred.

The men carry the sacred Grandmother Cedar out of the

lodge and set it up not far from "Grandfather Rock," a pillar of stone that represents the immovable foundation of the world. The pillar has been painted red, the color of life. So has the butt of the cedar.

Once the cedar has been set up near "Grandfather Rock," it will remain standing through the long winter until the first warm days of the following spring. Then the snow will melt; the ice will break on the Missouri River. Mothers will fasten to the branches of the cedar the worn moccasins of their little children. Grandmother Cedar will then be thrown into the flooding waters of the river.

Miles downstream, say the Arikara, the spirits of their ancestors will be watching. When they see how numerous are the children's moccasins tied to the floating tree, they will rejoice. They will know that the tribe is still powerful in the land.

The Pueblo Indians of the American Southwest use evergreen symbols—pine, spruce, or fir—for decorating their ceremonial costumes. Collars, armbands, belts, and kilts are decorated with these designs. Dancers often carry branches of spruce. Some Pueblo Indians bring evergreen trees from the forest and set them up in the dancing plaza. The feathers of birds may be fastened to the tips of the trees, much as the Arikara fasten hawk feathers to the crown of the Grandmother Cedar. These, again, are trees that "make the world green."

The Pueblo Indians believe, too, that a great fir tree grows in the underworld. This tree, they say, was the ladder on which, long ago, people climbed from the underworld to this earth where they now live.

The Book of Genesis in the Bible tells us that "the Lord God planted a garden eastward in Eden," and he made to grow there "every tree that is pleasant to the sight, and good for food; the tree of life also [was] in the midst of the garden, and the tree of knowledge of good and evil. And a river went out of Eden to water the garden. . . ."

The center of the garden was the center of the world to Adam and Eve; it was also the place where the tree of life grew. This tree was supposed to bring life without death to

all living things. Nearby grew the other tree, the tree of the knowledge of good and evil. The Lord God had forbidden Adam and Eve to eat its fruit. A serpent who was the devil himself persuaded Eve to eat the fruit of the tree. It tasted good, and she gave some to Adam.

Because they had disobeyed him the Lord God banished Adam and Eve from the Garden of Eden, and they never again saw the tree of life. From that time on there was death in the world, and evil. Adam and Eve and all their descendants were to know both of these things well.

The tree of life, however, has appeared all over the world. Often, as in the Aztec painting mentioned earlier, it has taken the form of a cross. A tree with branches on each side suggests a cross.

The cross on which Christ was crucified is often thought of as a tree of life. To Christians it brings hope that our life here on earth will not end with death. The New Testament says, "For as in Adam all die, even so in Christ shall all be made alive."

Everywhere the tree of life helped people to believe that no matter what might happen, life itself would continue. Evergreens would stay green through the silent cold of winter. And in springtime all the world would come alive again.

CHAPTER

6

*Sacred
Trees*

IT IS NOT surprising that people of long ago worshiped the trees that grew around them. Trees were the largest growing things, and they were always there. A man could see the same tree when he was a child, when he grew up, and when he was an old man. He knew that some of these trees were there when his father and mother, and his grandparents, too, were children. They might even be standing when his grandchildren grew old.

People felt that, like trees, they themselves kept on growing. Their bodies grew when they were children, but that was not all. Their minds and feelings grew as long as they lived, and there was a greatness within themselves that they called the soul. Trees reminded them of this. And because trees lived so many years people could hope that their own lives would somehow not end with death.

There were certain trees that were sacred; a spirit or a god was thought to live in them. People worshiped the gods of these sacred trees. In the valley of the Tigris and Euphrates rivers in Asia Minor, almost six thousand years ago, people carved on stone designs that represented their sacred trees. These designs were so beautiful that they were used as decorative sculpture on buildings in later times.

Sacred trees are important in many legends told by the people of ancient Greece. The oak was said to be the first tree to grow on earth; the Greeks called it "Mother Tree." Its acorns had been food for men in earliest times.

According to Greek mythology, a sacred oak at Dodona was sometimes inhabited by Zeus himself, the greatest of all the Greek gods. The oak, people said, was the tree most often struck by lightning. That was one reason Zeus the Thunderer dwelt in it.

People came to Dodona from all parts of Greece to ask Zeus, through his oak, to tell them what would happen in the future. The rustling and murmurs of the leaves of the tree were thought to be the words of the god himself. Priests interpreted these sayings for the people.

The myrtle was sacred to Aphrodite, Greek goddess of love and beauty. It was said that this tree could create love within a person and make it last.

Apollo, the Greek sun god, had a special feeling for the laurel tree, for reasons of his own. He had fallen in love with a beautiful nymph named Daphne, daughter of a river god. She would have nothing to do with him, but he kept pursuing her through the woods where she went hunting. One day as she ran frantically from Apollo she prayed the gods to let the earth open up and swallow her, or else change her to a different form, so Apollo would no longer pursue her. She held up her arms in prayer, and she was gradually covered with bark and leaves as she changed into a laurel tree. Apollo clasped the tree in his arms and vowed that it would be his favorite tree forever.

The Greek goddess Artemis was "lady of the wild things." She haunted mountains and meadows, took care of springs and rivers, and watched over little children. A sacred grove of trees was dedicated to Artemis.

Groves or forests were often considered sacred.

In ancient times people called Celts lived in western Europe and the British Isles. Their holy men were called Druids. The Druids told the people not to build temples to their gods or to worship their gods in any house or under any roof. The most sacred places of the Celts were groves and deep woods. Groves of oak trees were sometimes planted especially for worship. Each grove was watered by a sacred fountain or river. A ditch or a wall of earth surrounded the grove to keep out strangers. No one could enter except through a special passageway that was carefully guarded. In the center of the grove was a circular area enclosed by a row or two of large stones set upright in the earth. This was where the Celts worshiped their gods.

In India, one day very long ago, the great religious leader Gautama Buddha sat down under a bo tree (a kind of fig) on a cushion of freshly mown hay. He was determined to stay there quietly, thinking about the world outside himself and the world inside himself, until he gained true wisdom. He had looked many places in the world for this wisdom and had not found it. Now he knew he must find it within himself.

Throughout the night Gautama Buddha thought about everything that was happening to the living beings in the world. He thought of human suffering and of his own desire to help people find their way in life.

When dawn came Gautama Buddha had attained perfect wisdom. He stayed meditating beneath the bo tree for seven days. Legends grew up about this bo tree. It was supposed to be continually covered with heavenly flowers. The whole tree, even its smallest leaf, was said to be made of precious stones.

The bo tree brought a new way of life to Gautama Buddha. From that time on he devoted himself to helping people find the way to enlightenment, as he had found it under the bo tree.

In India the bo tree is still considered sacred by both Buddhists and Hindus. Every village where Buddhists live has its own bo tree near the temple. A branch of the original tree was planted more than two thousand years ago. It grew into a tree and is still growing, carefully tended by Buddhists of today.

Islam, the Muslim religion, began in Arabia more than a thousand years ago. The sacred book of the Muslims is the Koran, and it tells of a marvelous tree called Tooba that grew in paradise, in the seventh heaven. This tree was so big that the fastest horse could not gallop from one side of its shadow to the other in a hundred years. It shaded all of paradise. On its boughs hung delicious fruits unknown to people who live on earth. The souls in paradise could pick these fruits whenever they wished. At the foot of the tree ran a river of milk, a river of honey, and a river of wine, all for the pleasure of the inhabitants.

The Maoris, native people of New Zealand, believed that their god lived in giant trees called kauris. When they wanted one of these trees for a war canoe, they would first tell the god that they were much in need of his dwelling place. Trembling with fear, they would then cut down the great trunk. Each man was allowed to wear only one garment as he swung his stone ax, and he must not eat until his work was done.

People in many other parts of the world have believed in sacred trees, and this belief is not always a thing of the past. In Africa today people often worship their gods beneath a sacred tree or in a grove. The Bantu people hold some of their religious ceremonies at the foot of a tremendous fig. Its wide-spreading branches make a sort of roof that shades the people from the heat of the sun. Under it, the Bantus feel, they can worship their gods and be sure their gods will hear them.

A number of powerful Bantu spirits are thought to live in trees. In addition, each tree has a spirit-soul of its own. People bring gifts to the spirit of the tree so that he will not harm them. A Bantu hunter will leave beneath a special tree part of the game he has just killed. Then he and his family can enjoy their own share of the game without fear of trouble from the spirits.

In Peru in South America there is a bushy tree called the mastic. In earlier times this tree was sacred to the Inca Indians. To them it seemed a magic tree because such powerful medicines could be made from it. A brew made from its bark cured stomachache. A drink distilled from the juice of its berries calmed the nerves. Its leaves were used to make a tea that would relieve any kind of pain. White resin from the tree was helpful for reducing a swelling or curing an infection.

In many parts of the world poles and posts have been used in religious ceremonies or for magic. The poles are made of wood; they represent the tree from which they were cut. People believed that the spirit of the tree remained in the pole.

59

Some tribes of American Indians would set up a sacred pole in the center of their village. Or, if they moved often from place to place, they would take the pole with them, carefully wrapped. When they camped, they would set it up in a tent by itself. The spirit in the pole would watch over the people of the tribe.

The Omaha Indians lived on the Great Plains in what is now northeastern Nebraska. But at an earlier time they had lived farther east, in a land of meadows and forests. Their sacred pole was said to be the center of the four winds and the dwelling of the thunderbird.

The Omahas told a story about this pole. The first such pole came, long ago, from a miraculous cedar, at a time when two chieftains of the tribe had been quarreling about which one was most important. Some people favored one chief, some the other. It looked as if the tribe might be split in two.

One night the son of one of the chiefs went walking in the forest. Suddenly he saw before him a cedar that was all on fire, but was not being burned up. The trails of animals from the four directions of the world led to this cedar. Thunderbirds sat on its branches; they were like huge eagles and they could bring thunder, lightning, and rain.

The chief's son told the tribe what he had seen. The warriors put on the ornaments they used in war. They took their spears and ran shouting into the woods. There they cut down the miraculous tree and stripped off its bark. They brought

the tree into camp and adorned it as if it were a man, with a scalp at the top for its hair.

"You now see before you a mystery," said the chiefs. "We shall bring all our troubles to the Pole. We shall make offerings to it and ask its help. This Pole belongs to all the people."

And so the tribe was kept together.

Many tribes of Indians on the American Plains performed a great Sun Dance each summer. The dances differed from tribe to tribe, but in all of them the Sun Pole played an important part. This pole represented the universal idea of a tree that grows green when all the world grows green in springtime and summer.

The tree that was to become the Sun Pole had to be a growing cottonwood, straight and strong. On the first day of the ceremony a chosen hunter found a suitable tree and marked it with a circle of red paint. A buffalo dance was performed on this day, and there was a buffalo feast, but the chosen cottonwood remained where it grew. This was not its day.

On the second day the warriors of the tribe scouted about, looking for the chosen tree. On their fourth try they would find it. They taunted the tree and jeered at it. Then they bound it as if it were an enemy and left it standing there while they returned to camp with shouts of victory. The people sang songs of war and triumph. Why the tree was treated like an enemy we do not know.

62

A procession of people was then sent to bring in the captive. Four wise women, specially chosen for this task, cut down the tree while the people again shouted with joy. The bark was stripped off the tree up to the fork at its top, and men carried it in to the camp.

In the dancing lodge that had already been built the pole was painted with four vertical stripes—red for the West, blue for the North, green for the East, and yellow for the South.

On the third day the Sun Pole was finally set up. The people sang:

> *At the center of the Earth*
> *Stand looking around you!*
> *Recognizing the tribe*
> *Stand looking around you!*

Warriors danced the war dance. The Sacred Lodge was prepared for the great Sun Dance itself, which would take place the next day.

The warriors who did the Sun Dance fixed their eyes on the sun all day as they slowly circled the sacred pole. The dance was a kind of prayer. These people who were so close to the natural world could feel, again, that they lived in friendship with the spirits of nature and especially with the great Sun Spirit and the winds.

Camp was broken the day following the Sun Dance. The Lodge of the Sun Pole was destroyed before the people departed. The Sun Pole itself was left to stand alone until storm and wind sent it crashing down.

The Sun Pole was part of the great tradition of sacred trees all over the world. It seemed to the people that these trees told them about a power greater than themselves that brought new life to the world each year. They could feel this new life in themselves; they could see it in every green leaf.

CHAPTER

7

*Demons,
Dryads,
and
Fairies*

SUPPOSE you went for a walk by yourself in deep woods just at dusk. You would feel as if you were in another world. A twisted tree in the half light looks like some strange creature—a witch? Mists cling to the trunks of trees, then creep away like something alive. At first you feel you are surrounded by a vast silence. Then you realize that this is not silence after all. Leaves murmur all around you; they seem to be trying to say something to you. There is the slight sound of small creatures hurrying about. Then a sudden loud crash in the distance—what's THAT?

You would understand why earlier people believed that spirits inhabited the woods. Like them, you might imagine strange beings hiding among the trees.

The wood creatures of earlier times took on a variety of shapes and sizes—dryads, demons, fairies, elves. Some, like

66

the fairies, were merry folk. Others were mean and hateful; a person must keep out of their way at all costs.

In ancient Greece and Rome beautiful female creatures called nymphs were thought to live in such places as mountains, wild meadows, and forests. Wood nymphs were called dryads. They were lovely, gentle nymphs who wandered among the woods and danced around their sacred oak trees. Hamadryads, on the other hand, did not wander or dance. They were part tree themselves. Often they were imagined as being human from the waist up while their lower half was a tree trunk or roots.

The Greek gods often fell in love with beautiful dryads. Sometimes the dryads were pleased with this and sometimes not. The god Pan once took a dryad in his arms only to find she had changed herself to an armful of rough reeds.

Dryads and hamadryads often held axes to protect themselves and their special trees. A tree that was part of a hamadryad was said to bleed profusely when it was cut down. A cry of anguish would be heard, and then the hamadryad would die.

A man would be punished severely for cutting down such a tree. If the hamadryad did not succeed in bashing in his head with her ax, some other punishment would follow. One man who cut down a hamadryad's tree was punished by being made so hungry that he was never satisfied and finally even ate himself.

Wood nymphs were found in other countries, too. In Russia they had long green hair and they swung on the branches of trees in the forests.

The Czech people of central Europe tell a story about a wood nymph. This nymph roamed happily through the forest all day, but at night she returned to her special tree, a willow. A young man walking through the woods saw her and fell in love with her at once. The wood nymph said she could not marry him unless he would come to live near her willow. So he built a house for her there and became a woodsman. They were happy together and in time they had one child, a boy.

Then one day a man came into the woods with a great ax, looking for willow wood. Before anyone knew what was happening he had cut down the wood nymph's willow. She could not live without it and she died. Her husband chased the man who had cut down the tree all the way out of the woods with his own ax. Then he sat grieving for a day and a night on the trunk of the willow. After that he made a cradle of its wood. Whenever he rocked his child in the cradle, its wood lulled the child to sleep.

New twigs grew up around the stump of the willow tree, and when the boy became a man he made a pipe from one of these twigs. When he blew on it he was amazed to hear a voice speaking to him through the pipe. It was his mother's voice. After that they often talked together through the willow pipe.

Forests were thought to be the favorite haunts of fairies, especially in England and Ireland. They could be seen on any moonlit night, tiny creatures dressed in green, merrily dancing hand in hand around the trees. Grass where they had danced grew greener than before, and these green circles were called fairy rings.

Fairies were always ready to help mortals who were in trouble, though sometimes they played jokes, too. One joke was to get a man so confused that he could not find his way out of a field he had known all his life. To be released from this spell the man would have to turn his coat inside out.

In Scotland there was an ancient hawthorn tree that was supposed to be a meeting place for fairies. One day two young men were plowing the field where this tree grew. One of them drew a circle around the tree. "Here we must not plow," he said. At once a green table laden with bread, cheese, and wine miraculously appeared beside the tree. The young man who had drawn the circle sat down and ate and drank heartily. His companion, however, was scornful of the fairy food and kept on working. He would have done better to have accepted the fairies' gift, for from that time on his friend thrived as never before and became known far and wide for his wisdom.

70

Woodwives were rather sad little creatures who were believed to live in the woods of Germany and Scandinavia. They could be young and beautiful at one moment, old and ugly the next. Some people said they were lovely in front and hideous and hollow behind, with a tail they tried to hide. Woodwives were often hunted by a mythical character called the Wild Huntsman. To help the woodwives, foresters would cut three crosses on a tree they were cutting down. The little woodwives would sit in the center of the crosses. There they would be safe from the Wild Huntsman.

Woodwives often approached women who were baking and asked for a cake. They would beg woodcutters to mend their little wheelbarrows. In return for these favors they would change woodchips to gold. They loved to be with people and would weep bitterly if they were turned away. It was said that every time a young tree was twisted until the bark came off a woodwife would die.

In Germany it was believed that tiny elves roamed through the woods. They lived underground or in trees and could take on many different forms, such as that of butterflies or caterpillars. Some people thought that elves made the knotholes found in lumber.

People were careful not to offend the elves. They never spied on them or pried into their doings. An unfriendly elf could cause mysterious illnesses or even death. One old woman once tried to uproot a fir tree that was the home of an elf. The elf was so badly wounded that he died, and at that moment the old woman died also. From that time on, in the forests of Germany, old fir trees were cut off near the ground instead of being uprooted.

Fairies and elves were known in the woods of North America, too, though under Indian names. Mikamwes was an elf who frolicked in the moonlight in the vast American forests. Mischievous and lovable fairies called Mamagwasewug romped through the woods in Canada.

Demons and witches were something else again. No one expected anything but evil of them. Witches and demons of one form or another have cast their spell in all the forests of the world where people have lived.

In Russia the wood demon called Ljeschi was partly human, with the horns, ears, and feet of a goat. His fingers were claws, and his rough hair was green. He could make himself whatever size he chose. In the woods he might be as tall as the trees, in the fields no higher than the grass. He could look like a man clothed in sheepskins or appear as a beast with only one eye. When there was a storm in the woods Ljeschi would be seen springing from tree to tree, neighing and barking, trying to lead the traveler astray.

Indians who live in the jungles of the Amazon River in South America believe in a wood demon called Curupira. The Indians have never seen him, but whenever they hear a sound in the forest that is not made by a parrot, a howling monkey, or other familiar wildlife, they are sure that Curupira is about. They wander into his territory seldom, and then only in silence, full of dread.

On the other side of the world, in Japan, gnarled old trees with weird shapes were said to be the homes of wicked spirits who filled the woodsmen with dread. The most horrifying spirits, however, were the demons called Tengus who lived in the highest branches of tall trees. These demons were hatched from eggs. They had the body of a man, the head of a hawk, and the nose of a pelican.

In many places people were afraid to cut down trees because the demons of the woods might punish them severely in their wrath. In parts of Africa no man dared to go alone through the forest at night. The rustle of the leaves was the talk of demons conspiring against him. People could escape the evil influence of these demons by grasping certain magic roots.

In West Africa it was said that a demon dressed in scarlet clothing and named Sasabonsum attacked travelers in the forest at night and ate them. In the morning he sank into the ground, leaving the earth red from the blood of his victims.

Stories from around the world tell of a Wild Huntsman who rode furiously through the woods, causing great storms. It was he who harassed the little woodwives. In Germany it was said that the Wild Huntsman was the ghost of a mighty hunter who died in an accident. As he lay dying the parson urged him to think of heaven, but he refused. "The Lord may keep his Heaven," he said, "if I may keep my hunting." And so he was doomed to hunt in the forest until the end of time.

A distant baying of hounds was heard when the Wild Huntsman was on his way. A night owl called Tutosel flew before him. The owl screeched "Tu-hu!" while the Huntsman crashed along crying "Hu-hu!" Travelers in the woods fell silently on their faces as the Wild Huntsman passed by. Terror-stricken, they listened to the barking of the dogs and the weird "Hu-hu-Tu-hu!"

In the Scandinavian countries the Wild Huntsman rode a white horse and carried his head under his left arm. Coal-black hounds ran before him.

The Iroquois Indians of eastern North America called their Wild Huntsman Heno the Thunder. He rode on the clouds and split the trees of the forest with his thunderbolts.

Faraway in Asia, on the Malay Peninsula, a ghostly hunts-man was said to bring sickness and death to people as he ranged through the forests. Like the Wild Huntsman of Germany, he was accompanied by an owl, but this owl kept completely silent in the midst of the cry and clatter.

We have spoken of all the mythical forest creatures as if they belong to the past. But there are people today who say they have seen fairies dancing in the moonlight, and others

say they have heard the cry of the Wild Huntsman faraway in the forest. Still others are certain a demon pursues them when they walk in the woods at night. If you told them this could not be true, they would not believe you.

CHAPTER

8

Trees
for
Luck
and
Celebration

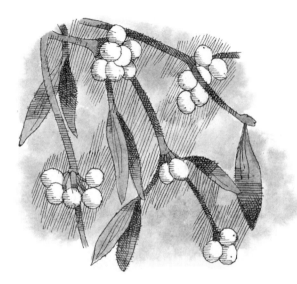

THERE ARE countless ways in which trees have been said to influence human life. A family in ancient Rome would plant a tree when a son was born. If the tree thrived, the family felt sure the son would be prosperous.

In ancient Palestine, too, a tree was planted when a child was born, a cedar for a boy, a cypress for a girl. As the children grew up they cared for their own trees. When they were married, the bridegroom and bride walked under a canopy made of branches cut from the trees that had been planted in their honor years before. People believed this would bring prosperity to the bride and groom.

In Mexico today there are Indians who plant a young tree at the time of the first new moon after a child's birth. They name the tree after the child, for good luck. These Indians are following an ancient custom of their ancestors, the Aztecs.

In many other places trees were thought to have considerable influence on marriage. In eastern Europe two trees were planted before the house of a newly wed couple. People said that if this was done, the husband and wife would be happy as long as they lived.

Trees could also help married couples to have many children. In the hill country of India, a bride and bridegroom would be married to two trees before being married to each other. The bride would clasp one tree trunk and the bridegroom another. A large family would surely result.

Marriage could help the trees themselves to bear fruit. On Christmas Eve German peasants used to tie two fruit trees together with straw rope. The trees were married, they said. Two such trees ought to produce a good crop.

The marriage of two trees was not unusual. In India, when a well-to-do Hindu planted a grove of mangoes, neither he nor his wife could eat the fruit until he married one of the trees to a tree of a different kind. He had to arrange an elaborate marriage ceremony for the trees. Hundreds of guests would be invited, and they would expect a feast. A procession of elephants, camels, and horses, all with gay trappings, was considered appropriate. The expense of such a wedding was great. A family might have to sell all its gold and silver trinkets in order to marry a mango tree to a jasmine.

Love was influenced by trees, too. In England people said the walnut tree could tell a young man who his true love

79

would be. First the young man must walk three times around the tree, saying, "Let her that is to be my true love bring me some walnuts." At once a spirit with his true love's face would be seen in the tree gathering nuts.

If a young man in Germany wanted his sweetheart to love him forever, he would choose a tree to represent himself. In a crack in the tree he would put three of his sweetheart's hairs. Her love for him would last as long as the tree lived.

Trees were believed to be useful in times of illness, too. In Germany it was said that a person could get rid of fever by putting some of his hair and nail clippings in a hole in a tree and then plugging up the hole. An easy way of getting rid of disease was for the sufferer to scrape it off by passing through a cleft in a tree. Children would be cured of illness if they were placed in a hole in a tree.

Trees were thought to be influential in still other ways. In Russia an old grove of sacred fir trees was supposed to bring rain. When rain was wanted, three men would climb one of the trees. The first man hammered on a kettle to imitate thunder. The second struck two burning sticks to make sparks fly, like lightning. The third sprinkled water from a bowl to imitate rain. After all this, sometimes it rained.

In England and Ireland the rowan tree, or mountain ash, was thought to be magic. "Rowan" came from an ancient word meaning "magic sign." It was said that the rowan tree could keep away evil spirits. If a branch of it was put in the butter churn or cheese vat, the butter or cheese would not be spoiled by witches. Old people used to put a branch of rowan on their pillows at night to keep away witches and evil spirits. A branch was hung over a baby's cradle on May morning for the same purpose. There are people who believe in the power of the rowan tree even today.

We often "knock on wood" to ward off some disaster. This is an ancient custom. Long ago, when a person wanted to ask a favor of the god who lived in a tree, he would touch the bark. If the favor was granted, he would thank the god by knocking on the tree. Touching certain trees was supposed to keep a person safe from harm. Today children echo this belief when they play tree tag, touching a tree to be safe from being caught.

For thousands of years trees have been a part of people's celebrations. In England, and sometimes in our own country, children, and grownups, too, dance around a maypole in the month of May. The maypole is a symbol of the new life that comes to the world when the long cold winter has ended.

Each person holds the end of a long streamer that has been fastened to the top of the maypole, and everyone then skips around the pole, moving in and out to weave the streamers together.

Sometimes they sing:

Round and round the maypole,
Merrily we go,
Tripping, tripping lightly,
Singing as we go.

This dance with weaving streamers is not a very old custom, but the maypole itself has a long history. It is a remnant of the worship of trees in early times.

In ancient Rome children wound garlands of flowers around a column in a temple. This was part of a festival called Floralia, in honor of Flora, goddess of flowers. The column represented a tree.

In Germany and Austria, a tall fir or spruce was brought to the village as a maypole. Branches and bark were removed from the lower part of the tree; the top was left green. People decorated the pole with flowers and colored ribbons, sometimes also with sausages, ham, and bottles of wine. They danced around their maypole. In country places this kind of May Day festival is often held today.

In England young people would go into the woods in the early morning hours on May Day. There they gathered the pink and white flowers of the hawthorn tree and carried

them home. This was called "bringing home the May." People decorated their doors and windows with these May blossoms. A lover would plant a branch of the hawthorn before his sweetheart's door.

Young people in England, like those in Germany and Austria, would cut down a tall tree in the woods and lop off all its branches except a few at the top. This was to be their maypole. It was sometimes as tall as a ship's mast. The maypole was carried to the village in a long wagon drawn by many pairs of oxen with garlands of flowers wound around their horns. Young people blew flutes and horns as the wagon carrying the maypole rolled along.

In the village, the pole was set up on the green. Sometimes it was painted with red and white stripes; these colors symbolized the springtime when all life on earth begins again. Everyone danced as the maypole was put up. Everyone sang. A May Queen came riding in a cart decorated with leaves and flowers and drawn by young men or maids of honor. On the village green the queen was crowned with a wreath of flowers. She represented the Spirit of Spring.

Poles have been a part of spring festivals in other places, too. In Burma, in Southeast Asia, there are people who dance around a special pole as part of their seedtime festival. In Switzerland young men plant May Pine Trees before their sweethearts' windows.

The Christmas tree also comes to us from the early days of tree worship, even though there was no Christmas then.

Long ago in ancient Egypt and Babylonia, people celebrated the time when the days began to grow longer after the shortest day of the year, on or about December 21. This is the winter solstice.

Winter in Babylonia and Egypt was not cold, as it is farther north. Even so, the passing of winter was a time to rejoice because the lengthening days gave promise that still warmer days would come and the eternal pattern of the seasons would be repeated once again. People celebrated with ceremonies and festivals. They decorated their houses with the leafy green branches of trees.

The Egyptians gathered branches of the date palm. This graceful tree flourished in the occasional green oases on the vast desert that lay beyond the valley of the Nile River. It told the Egyptians that life continues even when it is surrounded by death.

People in ancient Rome also decorated their houses with greenery at the winter solstice. In northern Europe fir trees and green boughs were brought home to remind people that the year had turned toward spring. In Germany the fir trees were hung with apples, sweet cookies, trimmings of gold and roses cut from many-colored paper.

None of these trees had anything to do with Christmas. That came later. No one knows the real date of the birth of

Christ, but in time a date was chosen for celebrating this great event. It seemed appropriate to place it near the time of the winter solstice. The lengthening of the days seemed a victory of light over darkness. Christians believed that the birth of Christ was a kind of victory, too, because Christ brought new hope to mankind.

People who had been celebrating the winter solstice for years adapted their festivals to the new holy day called Christmas. A story tells us that Martin Luther, the great German Protestant leader, decorated a little fir tree with lighted candles to represent the stars in the night sky. People liked the idea. Gradually it became the custom all over Germany to decorate a tree for Christmas.

Meanwhile people were beginning to travel to other countries in greater numbers than ever before. They took with them their own ideas and customs. The English people happily took over the Christmas tree from their German visitors. Before long the Christmas tree was known wherever people practiced the Christian religion.

Christians were celebrating the birth of Christ and the hope of new life to come. Often they did not know that long before Christ was born other people had also celebrated, with green boughs and decorated trees, the turn of the year toward spring.

Other miraculous trees came to be associated with this time of year. The famous "Glastonbury thorn" was one. It was a variety of hawthorn that blossoms late in the year wherever it grows. But legend said that the hawthorn at Glastonbury Abbey in England bloomed only on Christmas Day. This was indeed a wonderful happening; because of it, the tree was considered holy. Pilgrims came from far and wide to see the miraculous tree, and a branch cut from it was often carried in religious processions. The sale of blossoms and twigs from the tree became a profitable business. They were even shipped overseas to Christians in other countries.

The Glastonbury thorn no longer stands, but there are other hawthorns in England that grew from branches cut from it and planted long ago. They still put forth their fragrant white flowers during the shortest days of the year.

An old legend of Iceland tells of a mountain ash that was covered with bright lights on Christmas night. Even the strongest wind could not put out these lights, for they were the blossoms of the tree. It was sheer magic that brought them out on that night.

Trees have been a part of still other celebrations. In the southern part of Nigeria, in West Africa, a ceremony called Amofi is held every year around a special tree. The ceremony celebrates the escape of a former chief from great danger.

The chief was pursued by a whole crowd of fierce enemies. For days he managed to elude them by hiding in the forest. At last they discovered his hiding place and surrounded him.

He was desperate; there seemed to be no escape.

Just as the chief's enemies were about to close in on him, a magic cord dropped down from a tree and fastened itself around the chief. It lifted him up, up and whirled him into the treetops, out of sight. There he stayed, spinning at the end of the magic cord, while his pursuers thrashed about beneath, looking everywhere without finding him.

Finally the enemies gave up and went away. The magic cord gently lowered the chief to the ground, and he returned to his people and reigned happily over them for many years.

This miraculous escape happened long ago, but it is celebrated even today. On the morning of the important day the grass is cleared away around the special tree—a huge cottonwood—and long, thin cords made from forest vines are hung from the uppermost branches. In late afternoon the big drums begin to beat in a steady rhythm, calling the people to the ceremony. Hundreds of people gather, chatting together.

Then there is complete silence as the present chief arrives. He sits on a high throne where he can look over the heads of the people. Everyone gazes at the tree. Suddenly, as if from nowhere, two figures shoot out into the air from the topmost branches. They spin and spin, faster and faster, as they seem to float downward, shining, glistening in the sunlight.

For just a second the figures pause in midair, then they spin in the opposite direction, faster and faster, higher and higher, until they disappear in the treetop. And then again they spin, whirling down, pausing, whirling up to the treetop. And again. Everyone watches in silence, dizzy, feeling the spinning in themselves. Now and then a child spins himself around on one toe. Then suddenly there is a shower of leaves from the tree. Everyone rushes to catch a leaf, for good luck.

The figures that spin in the tree are two young men dressed in white, tight-fitting garments to which numerous small mirrors have been sewn. It is these mirrors that glisten in the sunlight. The cords from which the young men spin are so fine that they are invisible in the light of the sun.

The ceremony lasts only about fifteen minutes. But in that short time the people feel lifted out of their everyday lives, into the green spirit-world of the forest.

What event in your life would you like to celebrate? You can have your own celebration under your favorite tree. Sit there; look up into the branches. Think whatever thoughts you wish. Maybe all you want to celebrate is the happiness of sitting in green shade on a sunny day. Look. Think. For a little while you can be a part of the world of the tree.

CHAPTER

9

*Gifts
from
Trees*

TREES HAVE been useful to man ever since there were people on earth. From the wood of trees early people made weapons, such as clubs and bows and arrows, with which they hunted the animals of the forest for food. They made rafts of wood for traveling on streams. The sap of trees provided people with syrup, nuts that grew on trees gave them oil, and the fruit of trees fed them. Logs cut from trees were fuel for man's first fires.

Today we use trees in more ways than early people ever dreamed of. Yet some of the uses of trees have hardly changed at all. Our bodies still need the oxygen that is given off by all the green leaves in the world. And today, as always, people relish the fruits that grow on trees.

Over the centuries people have carried the seeds of fruit trees all around the world. As a result some fruits now grow thousands of miles from the places where they first grew wild. Oranges are one of the oldest fruits known to man, but they have been grown in North America for only a few hundred years.

More than four thousand years ago oranges grew wild in southern China and Indochina, and they were probably plentiful. We know this because oranges are mentioned in Chinese writings of that time. Then, at an unknown date, someone carried orange seeds, or perhaps small trees, to India. They flourished there. Arab traders took some seeds from India to Arabia and later to East Africa. Eventually orange trees reached Italy and Spain.

Christopher Columbus, on his second voyage to the New World, carried the seeds of both oranges and lemons to Hispaniola in the West Indies. There, too, orange trees flourished. Thirty years later it was said that they were "beyond counting." Soon they were also growing in South America, Mexico, and Florida. Spanish missionaries took oranges to California from Mexico and planted groves at their missions. Today most of our oranges grow in southern California and Florida where the climate is just right. Oranges and other citrus fruits cannot stand cold winters, but they must have cool nights during part of the year.

Apples have an even more varied history than oranges. Apple trees first grew in the cooler parts of Asia. The trees need to have winters that are cold enough to give them a rest from growing; otherwise they cannot produce fruit.

The fruit of the tree of knowledge in the Garden of Eden was supposed to have been an apple, but no one knows what it really was. It may have been an orange, a banana, a pomegranate, or a fig.

Apples reached parts of Europe a long time ago. Early people there cut some of their apples into pieces and sun dried them for use in winter. Dried apples have been found in the ruins of early towns in northern Italy and Switzerland.

By the time Christopher Columbus first sailed across the Atlantic Ocean, apples were the most important cultivated fruit in central and northern Europe. Spanish explorers who came after Columbus brought apples to the New World. People in England sent apple seeds to the Pilgrims of the Massachusetts Bay Colony in 1629. Apple trees thrived there. To be sure, a kind of apple had been growing in North America all the time, but it was a sour little crab apple growing on twisted trees.

When American pioneers began to go West, they took young apple trees with them. They were surprised to find apple trees already growing near Indian villages and in other places along the trails in the Middle West. Earlier white men had given seeds to the Indians.

Hundreds of orchards in Ohio and nearby areas were started in the early 1800s by one man—Johnny Appleseed. (His real name was John Chapman.) The story of Johnny Appleseed became a legend after his death.

Johnny was a friend to everyone, Indians and white peo-

ple alike. He traveled about, never staying long in one place. His hat was a tin pot, old cloth sacks served for his clothing, and he wore no shoes at all. In the evening a farm family would see his small bearded figure coming up the road. They would invite him to have supper and stay the night. The children especially looked forward to his coming; they knew he would tell them a story after supper. Sometimes, too, Johnny would talk to the whole family about the love of nature and of all mankind.

Over his shoulder Johnny carried a bag containing apple tree seedlings and apple seeds. Wherever he went he scattered apple seeds, gave them to the settlers to plant, or left seedlings with them, little apple trees that had already been started. In the fields and woods where he roamed you can still find spicy apples on trees descended from those planted by Johnny Appleseed. His apples will still be growing, on other trees, hundreds of years from now. And his legend will still be told.

Other favorite fruit trees had their beginnings in far countries. Peaches, like oranges, first grew wild in China. The Chinese said that peaches had magic powers; anyone who ate them would never die. Or if it was too late to prevent death, the fruit would at least keep a person's body from decaying.

Peach trees also traveled westward. The Greeks grew them about two thousand years ago. The trees were brought to North America by the earliest settlers.

96

Pears were a very special fruit to the ancient Greeks. They held a festival of pears in the spring; and the Greek poet Homer wrote about pears in his *Odyssey*. Early pear trees grew wild in southwestern Asia, but it was cultivated varieties that were brought by the settlers to America.

Cherries have a long history, too. They grew wild in both the Old World and the New World long before the time of Columbus, but they were first cultivated in China. A cultivated variety of cherry trees arrived in the New World on the Mayflower.

The list of fruits enjoyed by people is a long one. Some fruits that were eaten in former times are no longer relished by most people. Early people often ate acorns; so did the American Indians. Few people today have tried acorns, though acorns are said to be quite tasty when they are boiled and dried and dipped in sugar syrup.

At times other parts of trees have been eaten. The Indians of the northwestern part of North America ate the powdered bark of the tamarack tree. If you live in the country, you may have chewed the sweet-tasting bark on twigs of the black birch. This is a favorite food of native people in northeastern Siberia. A delicious syrup can be made from the sap of black birch as well as from the sap of the maple tree.

Starch taken from the spongy center of the sago palm makes a good pudding. Palm tree buds are tasty in salad.

Coffee beans are the seeds of the coffee tree, a plant which first grew wild in the part of Africa now called Ethiopia. For a long time no one thought of using these beans for any purpose at all. Then a priest visiting in Arabia watched a goat nibbling the leaves of the coffee tree. The goat seemed unusually gay and full of energy. The priest tried nibbling the leaves, too, and he felt like dancing. Later it was discovered that coffee beans make an even better beverage than the leaves, and the custom of drinking coffee spread around the world.

Then there is the chocolate tree, or the cacao. This tree grows wild in Mexico and Central America. The Aztec Indians of Mexico were fond of sipping chocolate, which they made from the seeds, or beans, of the cacao tree. We drink it, too, and we also put chocolate in ice cream and candy and cookies and cake.

Medicine has long been made from trees. Sometimes trees were even supposed to cure disease by magic; we have seen examples of this in the preceding chapter. But many trees have proved helpful to sick people quite without magic.

When the Frenchman Jacques Cartier was exploring the Saint Lawrence River in the year 1536, twenty-six of his men died of a disease called scurvy. Many of his other men were desperately sick with the same disease. Indians cured them by giving them a tea made from green spruce needles. Scurvy is caused by a lack of vitamin C in the diet, and the spruce tea supplied this. Cartier and the Indians did not know why the remedy worked; to them it may have seemed like magic.

The American sassafras is another tree that gained an early reputation for curing sickness. Sassafras tea was made from the roots. A writer of the sixteenth century stated that the tea had "power to comfort the liver—to comfort the weake and feeble stomacke." Drinking sassafras tea became popular even with people who did not have weak stomachs. One of the first ships that carried a cargo from America to Europe was loaded with sassafras roots, along with cedar logs.

A lotion for the skin can be brewed from the bark of still another tree—the witch hazel. Witch hazel lotion is soothing when it is rubbed on a sprained ankle or on an itchy mosquito bite.

Oils from many trees soothe irritated skin. The oil that the Good Samaritan of the Bible story poured into the wounds of the traveler who lay by the side of the road was probably the oil of olives. Eucalyptus oil is used today for minor infections of the nose and throat. A soothing oil from the bark of the slippery elm is often put into cough drops. This same bark was also once known as a cure for scurvy. It could be chewed or ground into flour.

In India grows a useful tree called the nim. Its flowers are like tiny white and yellow stars clinging to long drooping stems. These change to yellow fruit about the size of small olives. Oil from this fruit is used to treat diseases of the skin.

In the past, bark of trees was often made into clothing. The native people of the Hawaiian Islands pounded the inner bark of certain trees, such as paper mulberry, until it was soft, thin, and flat. This made a cloth called tapa. Designs were stamped or painted on tapa cloth, and it became a thing of beauty.

The most luxurious fabric in the world is silk. Though silk thread does not come directly from a tree, it could never have been woven into cloth if there were no mulberry trees. The worms that make silk will eat nothing but the leaves of the mulberry.

Mulberries grew wild in China long before they were used by people to feed the worms that make silk. There is an old Chinese legend that tells how silk cloth was invented, thousands of years ago. It all began in the garden of a Chinese emperor. The lovely Empress Si Ling-Shi sat drinking tea one day under a mulberry tree in her garden. She gazed up into the tree and saw a fat white worm moving its head back and forth. A shiny gold-colored thread came from the worm's mouth. The thread became longer and longer as the worm wrapped it round and round itself to make a shining and beautiful cocoon.

The young empress wondered how she would look dressed in the threads of many of these cocoons. She plucked the cocoon from the mulberry tree and dropped it into her tea. There it became soft, and the empress took hold of one end of the thread and carefully unwound it.

The empress then persuaded her husband to give her a whole grove of mulberry trees. She spent years working with the worms and cocoons before she had enough thread to weave cloth. This was the beginning of silk.

No one knows whether this story is true. But for more than two thousand years the Chinese carefully guarded the secret of making silk. No one else knew how to make it. Today, though the worms cannot live in cold climates, silk is made in many other countries.

Another substance that is made by an insect living on trees is lac, from which shellac is made. Tiny scaly insects attach themselves by the hundreds of thousands to the twigs of certain trees in the tropics. They suck the sap from the trees and at the same time give off lac as a protection against enemy insects and the weather. Lac covers the insects like a blanket.

People gather lac from the twigs; a single pound of it is the life work of some one hundred fifty thousand insects! The lac is purified and finally dissolved in alcohol to make the shellac that is so often used as a finish on wood floors and furniture.

For thousands of years people have made many things directly from wood—houses, furniture, and all sorts of useful objects, from baseball bats to railroad ties. The American Indians made dugouts by burning out the inside of a big tree trunk and smoothing it with shells or stone tools. Indians of eastern North America made their canoes of birch bark. Trees furnished the materials for their bows and the shafts of their arrows.

All these things that were made of wood still looked like wood. But today there are countless things made from wood that do not look as if they ever came from a tree. Your imitation leather jacket may be made from wood. You can drive on wood, because the strong rayon cord in tires is made from wood pulp. So is the rayon that is used in clothes. You can take a picture with wood pulp; photographic film is made from it. You can drink from a plastic cup made from wood and blow your nose on wood pulp that has been made into paper tissue.

When you eat an apple nothing happens to the tree it came from. It will live to grow more apples another year. The same is true of all trees that give us fruit and many other things. But when logs are burned in a campfire or fireplace they are changed to ashes and the tree or the tree branch they came from no longer exists. Lumber also uses up trees; so does paper made from wood pulp. You cannot make anything with wood and save the tree the wood came from.

That is why the foresters who provide wood for today's countless uses must take good care of trees. The supply is not endless. Some forests can renew themselves if too many trees are not cut down. The trees that are left standing produce seeds that grow new trees, even if none are planted by people. But often trees must be planted to replace those that are gone. Enough must be planted so that we will have wood for all our future needs.

Think of these things as you sit in the shade of your favorite tree. Eat an apple or an orange. Imagine drinking sassafras tea. Consider how many things you are wearing may have been made from wood.

Your tree was probably pushing its roots into the earth long before you ever sat beneath it. Will it still be there a hundred years from now? No one knows. Depending on where it is, it may be cut down, bulldozed down, or chopped up and hauled away. Or it may stand and grow for many years, until it slowly dies and a woodpecker makes his home in a hole in the trunk—another good use for a tree.

CHAPTER
10

*Plant
a
Tree*

THERE IS a story about a tree told in the Talmud, the ancient Jewish book of laws and tradition.

One day a man named Honi saw an old man digging a hole in the earth.

Honi said to the old man, "At your age, must you do this heavy work? Have you no sons to help you?"

The old man kept on digging. "This I must do myself," he said.

Honi asked, "But how old are you?"

"I am seventy years and seven," the old man answered.

"And what are you planting?"

"I am planting a bread tree," said the old man. "The fruits of this tree can be ground to flour and used as food for many."

"When will it bear fruit, your tree?" asked Honi.

"In seventeen years and seven."

"But you will surely not live that long," said Honi.

"No," said the old man, "I will not live that long. But I must plant this tree. When I came into this world, it was not a desolate place. I found trees and bread. I must not leave this a desolate world, but a world with trees growing. Our fathers planted trees, and so must we."

The "bread tree" the old man planted was a carob, a tree that grows in the lands around the Mediterranean Sea. Its fruit is like beans encased in long brown pods. Today this fruit is sometimes called "Saint-John's-bread." The flour made from it is a delicious food.

The old man in the story was planting a tree that had already started growing. We know this because he had to dig a sizable hole in the earth. Most trees are planted this way. Often they are started in tree nurseries. Or small trees may be dug up in the wild and then planted where people want them. Lumber companies often start new forests by planting thousands of little trees in areas where they have cut down most of the big trees.

Every tree in the world started with a seed or a cutting from a big tree. The "beans" of the carob tree are its seeds. Acorns grow on an oak tree and are its seeds. When an acorn is ripe it falls to the ground. It may be eaten by a squirrel. But suppose no squirrel finds it, and suppose no child puts it in his pocket and carries it home. In the fall, dead leaves cover the ground where the acorn lies. Snow covers the leaves in winter. The acorn stays in the cold darkness beneath the leaves all winter.

Then spring comes. The sun warms the leaves and the acorn and the soil. Rain and melting snow moisten the acorn. It starts to change. A little root pokes out and finds its way into the ground. Two tiny leaves on a stem grow up toward the light. The little tree grows and grows. It will be years before it is a big oak tree, but it has made a beginning.

Trees do not always grow up near their parent tree. A squirrel may carry away an acorn, bury it, and never find it again. Another oak tree grows. Birds eat wild fruits, such as cherries, and may drop the seeds. Or the seeds may pass through the birds and fall to the ground wherever the birds happen to be. More trees grow. Some seeds, such as the winged seeds of maple, are carried by the wind, and where they fall to the earth some will sprout and maples will grow.

We have seen how trees were often planted when a child was born, or when a couple was married. This was done for good luck. In many parts of the world people have believed that good luck would come to anyone who planted a tree.

Elzeard Bouffier had his own reasons for planting oak trees all over the hills near his native village in France. Bouffier spent his days taking care of his sheep while they grazed on those hills. Most of the time the sheep just walked about and ate grass. Bouffier had plenty of time to watch them, and

he did not like what he saw. There were too many sheep. They nibbled the grass and other vegetation right down to the ground. Their sharp hooves cut into the plants that were just starting to grow.

Before long there was almost nothing growing on the hills where Bouffier grazed his sheep. Wind blew clouds of dust over the unsheltered land. The hills were becoming a desert. Only a handful of people remained in the nearby village.

Bouffier knew then what he wanted to do more than anything else in the world. He would plant trees. He collected thousands of acorns from a forest on the other side of the hills. Every day, year after year, he put one hundred acorns in a sack, carried them up into the hills, and planted them. Not all the acorns sprouted. Some that did sprout and grow were eaten by animals, and some did not survive the winter. But many grew.

Meanwhile Bouffier kept his sheep in the valley, with a dog to watch, and he sold a few sheep at a time until he had only four. Instead he kept one hundred beehives, and the bees made honey. In ten years or so the oak trees he had first planted were taller than Bouffier. He could walk all day in his forest. By this time he was planting not only oaks but beech trees, and birches along the streams in the valleys.

Twenty years after Elzeard Bouffier began to plant acorns the government of France sent a delegation to see his forest. They put it under state protection. People came to live in the village. There were farms and fields and houses and flowers. Elzeard Bouffier had built a countryside by planting trees.

Trees are cut down by the thousands in our own country every day—for lumber, for paper, to make way for highways and buildings. But trees are being planted here, too. In many places throughout the country groups of children plant trees. Some are Boy Scouts or Girl Scouts, some are Future Farmers of America, others belong to 4-H Clubs. They plant wherever trees are needed. Sometimes they help restore a forest that has been burned. They work with the United States Forest Service and local groups. And they take care of the trees they have planted, watching them, watering them.

Planting trees with a group can be a game or a race to see who can plant the most. But the young people are proud of what they have done when they see their forest growing. And they hope that some of the trees will still be standing for their children and grandchildren to see.

If you can, with someone to help you, plant a little tree in your own back yard. Remember that a tree grows big! Choose a place where it will have room to grow. Water it every week the first year, except when there is a heavy rain. Watch it. Cherish it.

There are tree-planting programs in most big cities in the United States. In New York City trees are planted not only by the city, but by private citizens. If you want to plant a tree along a New York City street you must first get permission from the Department of Parks. They will make sure you have chosen a good place for your tree, and they will suggest a variety that should do well in the city. It might be a ginkgo, a London plane, a honey locust, a willow oak, or a silver linden.

You will not be allowed to do the actual planting yourself. Your tree must be planted by a nursery. They will not only be sure to plant it properly but will stake it and take care of it for the first year. If you really want your tree, you will have to pay for all this, and it costs about one hundred fifty dollars for a London plane or one hundred seventy-five dollars for a ginkgo.

People *do* want trees. In Manhattan, which is only one part of New York City, a thousand trees are planted every year by people who pay for them.

New York City also has a "Street Tree Match Program." Block associations and other local groups contribute two hundred dollars toward the cost of four trees. The city "matches" their contribution with another six trees. These trees are planted by the city, but the people in the group can choose the kind they want.

San Francisco has a "Plant a Tree Week" every year in March. School children make posters about tree planting. All the posters are exhibited in a big department store, and some win prizes. The children are learning to care about the trees in the streets.

The climate in San Francisco is much warmer than New York City's climate. Different trees can be planted. A resident of San Francisco might choose, among others, a carob or an Australian tea tree or a Brazilian pepper. Or, just because it is a fascinating tree wherever it grows, he might choose a ginkgo.

Trees in cities often have a hard time. If they are planted along a sidewalk, they usually have only a small square of earth around them, and this is packed down hard by rain and by people's feet. Only a little water can soak in. It helps if someone will loosen the earth around a tree now and then in summer and slowly pour in several pails of water. During a dry spell, pour in six pails, twice a week.

Many trees will not stay green in the smoggy air of cities. They do not thrive on dog manure and urine. They need more pruning and other kinds of care than they usually get.

Newly planted trees and shrubs may be stolen from city parks. People dig them up at night and cart them away. In New York City the Department of Parks finally chained the trees they planted to horizontal underground stakes. Thieves tried to dig up the chained trees, but they did not succeed.

Difficult though it is, we must keep on trying to grow trees in cities. People want them. When *Life* magazine asked a number of people what they wanted most, a large majority said they wanted a place where they could sit on green grass under a tree.

President Theodore Roosevelt once said, "A people without children would face a hopeless future; a country without trees is almost as hopeless."

That is how the people of Nebraska felt when their state legislature set up Arbor Day in 1872. Settlers had cut down most of the trees in Nebraska as they cleared the land for farming, built their homes, and cut firewood. A person could travel for miles without seeing a single tree. Much of the state was a wasteland. Trees were needed for lumber and firewood, to act as windbreaks, and to help hold the moisture in the soil. People also wanted trees for shade and beauty.

A prize of one hundred dollars was offered by the state legislature to the county agricultural society that planted the most trees. The individual who planted the most received a library of books about farming.

The first year, a million trees were planted in Nebraska. Within sixteen years, the total was six hundred million. Wasteland was changing to forest.

As time went on, Arbor Day was observed in other states, and it was finally recognized in all of them. The date varies in different places, but it is usually a day in March or April. The last Friday in April is Arbor Day in Chicago. There are programs in all the parks. In downtown Grant Park a thousand little trees are given away to people who gather for the Arbor Day program. These are their own trees, to plant wherever they wish.

Most of all, Arbor Day is a time when school children plant trees. They read poems, sing, and put on plays about trees. Sometimes they plant a tree in honor of a famous person who also loved trees—such as Johnny Appleseed. Like the old man in the story from the Talmud, the children want this to be "a world with trees growing."

A special day for growing trees was a new idea in Nebraska, but special tree plantings have been carried out in other places for centuries. The Spanish people have had their own version of Arbor Day for many years. Boys plant saplings and tend them carefully. In Switzerland, people would sometimes decide they wanted a grove of oaks near their village. On a certain day each year they would go into the woods, dig up a young oak tree, and bring it back to the village. The tree would be planted in a chosen spot, and after a few years the people would have their grove.

The Jews in Israel celebrate a New Year of Trees, Tu Bishebat. This is an ancient springtime holiday, held at the time when the sap rises in the trees and myriads of wild flowers blossom on the hillsides. Centuries ago Jewish farmers planted trees and blessed their orchards on this day. Now, Israeli children parade through the streets, carrying spades, hoes, and watering cans. Later they plant trees in the fields or along the streets. They are planting not just for themselves but for all the people who will come after. Trees have been planted for so many years that in some places no more are needed. But people celebrate just the same. Trees planted in former years are pruned and watered. Little trees are moved to new locations.

After the work is done the fun begins. Children dance and sing and go on hikes. Grownups feast on the good fruits that grow in Israel—figs, dates, almonds, and the beanlike fruit of the carob tree.

Trees are especially important in Israel. There is little rain and the land is dry. Trees must be planted and watered carefully if they are to grow. Then they can help to hold the dusty soil in place.

CHAPTER
11

*Save
a
Tree*

NOT EVERYONE can plant a tree. Not everyone wants to. Sometimes it is enough just to save a tree that is about to be destroyed.

In Dedham, Massachusetts, a town meeting was held not long ago to discuss the widening of a street. More cars could use the street if it was widened by ten feet on each side. A fifteen-year-old resident of the street objected to the plan. There was a tree in front of his house, he said, one of the few remaining at his end of the block. He did not want it cut down just to make way for more trucks and cars. He would rather see grass and trees than concrete. The people at the meeting listened to the boy. And they voted, one hundred thirty-three to ninety-eight, against the plan to widen the street.

On a street in Brooklyn, New York, children helped save a beautiful magnolia tree. This was a variety of magnolia that is usually found only in the South. It had been growing in front of brownstone houses in the Bedford-Stuyvesant section of Brooklyn for eighty-five years, the biggest and oldest tree of its kind in the North. In summer it was covered with large, fragrant, creamy-white flowers. The people in the neighborhood loved it.

Then the city decided to tear down the houses on the block and build a housing development. They wanted the area behind the tree for a parking lot. Without the brownstone houses to shield it, the tree would be blown and buffeted by cold winds in winter. It would almost certainly die.

A group of determined citizens decided that the tree should not die. They formed the Magnolia Tree Committee, led by a grandmother, Mrs. Hattie Carthan. Many people offered to help. Articles about the tree appeared in newspapers all over the country and overseas. The Horticultural Society of New York offered to give five thousand dollars toward saving the tree if the committee could raise an equal amount.

The committee came up with the idea of selling raffle tickets in the shape of a tree, five leaves apiece, all five for a dollar. Children sold tickets. Neighborhood businesses gave money. Altogether they raised seven thousand dollars. The New York Landmarks Preservation Committee designated the tree a living landmark, to be preserved. The committee celebrated with a big party, a Celebration of Life.

"The tree stands high and mighty and beautiful for us," Mrs. Carthan said.

But it was not certain that it would continue to stand. The Magnolia Tree Committee wanted to use the houses behind the tree as an Earth Center for Nature Studies for the young people of the community, but the builders of the housing development refused for a long time to change their plans. The committee kept on working. Finally the builders agreed to leave the three brownstones standing. And the housing development was named Magnolia Plaza.

Trying to save the magnolia tree led to many other community activities. There was a Seed Hunt every autumn. Children collected the bright red seeds of the magnolia and gave them to the Horticultural Society. More magnolia trees would grow from the seeds. Children joined a neighborhood Tree Corps; they took care of trees that were planted along the streets and learned about how things grow. Every now and then the Magnolia Tree Committee had a special tree-planting ceremony, a "plant-in."

Trees were growing in Brooklyn.

In Virginia, near Washington, D.C., high school students helped save a woods that was to be cut down to make way for new houses. They worked hard, going from door to door talking to people about the woods, getting the people to sign petitions. They wrote to local newspapers; they were interviewed on television. And they won. The townspeople voted to buy the land for a park.

Sometimes trees *do* have to be cut down. We must have lumber for houses, trees for making paper and many other

things. And sometimes trees are in the way. They may have been planted so close to a house that when they grow big they shut out most of the light inside the house. Then the homeowner must decide whether he wants light in his house or a tree outside his window.

Often, though, when houses are built on new land, all the trees are bulldozed down indiscriminately. Shopping plazas are cleared by ripping up trees, some of which could be saved. Trees that have been growing for centuries cannot be replaced.

Just one tree in a bare space can make a place beautiful. Just one good-sized healthy tree produces enough oxygen in one growing season to keep one person alive for a year. We need trees.

Perhaps you do not believe that trees are inhabited by spirits. For you no tree holds knowledge of good and evil, no bo tree brings true wisdom. You do not hear strange voices in the forest; you hear no "Hu-hu!" of a Wild Huntsman. For you no fairies dance in moonlit woods, no woodwife begs for a cake.

Still, you may dance with joy around your Christmas tree. You may sit in the shade of a tree and dream that you are growing upward, as the tree grows. And perhaps you can plant a tree or save a tree. Then you will be one of the millions of people who, ever since man walked the earth, have cherished this green world.

Books
for
Further
Reading

NOTE: most of the following books were written for children. Included also are a few adult books which may be of interest to older children.

Collis, John Stewart, *The Triumph of the Tree*. New York: The Viking Press, Inc., 1960. (Paperback; adult book.)

Cormack, Maribelle B., *The First Book of Trees*. New York: Franklin Watts, Inc., 1951.

Cosgrove, Margaret, *Plants in Time*. New York: Dodd, Mead & Co., 1967.

——— *Wonders of the Tree World* (revised). New York: Dodd, Mead & Co., 1970.

Crispo, Dorothy, *The Story of Our Fruits and Vegetables*. New York: Dorex House, 1968. (Adult book.)

Dudley, Ruth H., *Our American Trees*. New York: Thomas Y. Crowell Company, 1956.

Farb, Peter, and the Editors of *Life*, *The Forest* (Life Nature Library). New York: Time/Life Books, Time Inc., 1963. (Adult book.)

Fenton, Carroll Lane, and Herminie B. Kitchen, *Fruits We Eat*. New York: The John Day Company, Inc., 1961.

Fenton, Carroll Lane, and Dorothy Constance Pallas, *Trees and Their World*. New York: The John Day Company, Inc., 1957.

Hutchins, Ross E., *This Is a Tree*. New York: Dodd, Mead & Co., 1964.

Lane, Ferdinand C., *The Story of Trees*. New York: Doubleday & Company, 1953. (Adult book.)

Lehner, Ernst, and Johanna, *Folklore and Symbolism of Flowers, Plants and Trees*. New York: Tudor Publishing Co., 1960. (Adult book.)

Lemmon, Robert S., *Junior Science Book of Trees*. Champaign, Illinois: Garrard Publishing Co., 1960.

Milne, Lorus, and Margery, *Because of a Tree*. New York: Atheneum Publishers, 1963.

Selsam, Millicent E., *Play with Trees*. New York: William Morrow & Co., Inc., 1950.

Webber, Irma E., *Thanks to Trees*. New York: William R. Scott, Inc., 1952.

White, Florence M., *Your Friend, the Tree*. New York: Alfred A. Knopf, Inc., 1969.

Index

Acorn, 55, 97, 107–8, 110
Adam and Eve, 51–52
Africa, 98; life trees, 43–44; pygmies, 19–22; sacred trees, 58–59; tree ceremonies in, 87–89; wood demons in, 73
Ainu people, 45
Alder: life tree, Ireland, 43
Animals and world trees, 27, 28, 30, 31, 36
Aphrodite, sacred tree of, 55
Apollo, laurel tree and, 55–56
Appleseed, Johnny, 94–96, 115
Apple tree, 93–96
Arabia, 58, 98
Arbor Day, 114–16
Arikara Indians, 48–49
Artemis, sacred grove of, 56
Ar-tojon, god of heaven, 38
Asgard mountains, 28, 31
Ash: life tree, Greek, 43; life tree, Ireland, 43; life tree, Scandinavian, 43; mountain, Iceland, 87; rowan, English and Irish magic tree, 80–81; world tree, Scandinavian, 27–32, 34, 37
Ashanti people, 43–45
Asia, 93, 97; world trees, 36–37
Asia Minor: sacred trees, 55; world trees, 27, 35–36
Askr, Scandinavian life tree, 43

Austria, maypoles in, 84
Aztec Indians, 98; life tree, 46–48, 52; trees for luck, 78; world tree, 40

Babylonia, 85
BaMbuti Pygmies, 19–22
Bantu people: sacred tree of, 58–59
Bark, 37, 97, 99, 100, 102
Bible, 99; trees in, 35–36, 51–52
Birch, 14, 97
Birds: and life trees, 45, 46–47; and world trees, 28, 30, 34, 35
Bouffier, Elzeard, 108–11
Branches, 11, 12, 18, 26, 27, 34, 35, 36, 40, 81, 85
Brooklyn, N.Y., 118–20
Buddha, Gautama: bo, sacred tree of, 57–58
Buddhist world tree, 35
Burma: poles in, 84

Cacao (chocolate) tree, 98
California, 93
Canada: elfs in, 72
Carob (bread) tree, 106–7
Cartier, Jacques, 98
Cassia, Chinese world tree, 36
Cedar: boys in Palestine, 78; life tree of

Arikara Indians, 48–49; sacred tree of Omaha Indians, 60, 62
Celebrations, trees in, 81–89
Celts: sacred groves of, 56
Cherry tree, 97
China, 96, 97, 100–1; world tree of, 36
Christmas tree, 86–87
Coffee tree, 97–98
Columbus, Christopher, 93, 94
Conservation of trees, 118–22
Cottonwood: American Indian sun pole, 62–64
Cross: as life tree symbol, 52
Curupira, wood demon, 72–73
Cypress: girls in Palestine, 78
Czechoslovakia: wood nymphs in, 68–70

Daniel, Book of, 35–36
Daphne, Greek nymph, 55–56
Dedham, Mass., 118
Demons, wood, 66, 72–76
Dodona, Greece: sacred tree at, 55
Dragons, 36, 37, 40
Druids: sacred groves of, 56
Dryads (wood nymphs), 66, 67–70

Eagle, 28, 30, 35, 37
Egypt: soul-tree, 45–46; winter solstice celebrations, 85
Elm: life tree, Scandinavian, 43; slippery elm, oil from, 99
Elves, 66, 71–72
Embla, Scandinavian life tree, 43
England: ash, magic tree, 80–81; fairies in, 70; May Day hawthorn flowers, 82–84; maypoles in, 84; trees and love, 79–80
Ethiopia, 98
Eucalyptus, oil of, 99
Euphrates River, 27, 55
Evergreens, 11, 23, 38, 52, 71–72, 82, 86; life trees of Pueblo Indians, 49, 51

Fairies, 66, 67, 70, 72
Fig tree: Bantu sacred tree, 58–59; bo, sacred tree of Gautama Buddha, 57–58; life tree, African, 45; sycamore, Egyptian soul tree, 45
Fir trees, see Evergreens
Flora, 82
Florida, 93
Food from trees, 19, 23, 55, 92
Forests, 38; BaMbuti Pygmies in, 19–22; early man and, 18–19, 22–24; fairies in, 70; mysteries and fears of, 21–23; sacred, 56; Wild Huntsman in, 71, 73–74, 76; woodwives in, 71
Fruit trees, 19, 23, 34–35, 36, 92–97, 107

Garden of Eden: trees of life and knowledge in, 51–52, 94
Genesis, Book of, 51–52
Germany: elves in, 71–72; fir tree, Christmas, 86; maypoles in, 84; trees and marriage, 79; trees and illness, 80; trees and love, 80; Wild Huntsman, 73–74; winter solstice celebrations, 85; woodwives in, 71
Glastonbury hawthorn, 86–87
Greeks, 96, 97; dryads and hamadryads, 67; life tree, 43; sacred trees, 55–56
Groves, sacred, 56
Growth, 11–12, 107–8

Hamadryads, 67
Hawthorn: English, 86–87; flowers on May Day, 82–83
Hazel, witch, 99
Heno, Iroquois Indian Wild Huntsman, 74
Hereros people, 43
Hindus: sacred tree of Gautama Buddha, 57–58; tree marriages, 79; world tree, 34–35

Ice Age, 18–19
Iceland: mountain ash, 87
Illness, trees and, 59, 80
Inca Indians, sacred tree of, 59
India: sacred trees, 57–58; tree marriages, 79; world trees, 34–35
Indians, American, 94, 97, 98–99, 101–2;

fairies and elves, 72; life trees, 48–49, 51; sacred poles, 60–64
Indians, South American: wood demon of, 72–73
Insects, 100–1; and life trees, 45
Ireland: ash, magic tree, 80–81; fairies in, 70; life trees, 43
Iroko (African Oak), life tree, 43
Iroquois Indians: Wild Huntsman, 74
Islam, sacred tree of, 58
Israel: New Year of Trees, 115–16
Italy, 94
Ituri Forest, 19–22

Japan: life tree, 45; wood demons in, 73; world tree, 36

Kalpadruma, world tree, 34
Kauris, sacred tree of Maoris, 58
Knocking on wood, 81
Koran, 58

Lac tree, 101
Laurel, sacred tree of Apollo, 55–56
Leaves, 10–11, 12, 15, 27, 36, 37, 38, 64, 92
Lemon tree, 93
Life, trees of, 42–52; African, 43; American Indians, 48–49, 51; cross symbol, 52; Egyptian, 45–46; Garden of Eden, 51–52; Greek and Roman, 43; Ireland, 43; Mexico, 46–48, 52; Scandinavian, 42–43
Ljeschi, Russian wood demon, 72
Love, trees and, 79–80, 84
Luck, trees and, 78–81, 89, 108
Lumber, 102–3, 107, 111

Magnolia: Brooklyn campaign to save, 118–20
Mamagwasewug, Canadian elf, 72
Man, origin of in trees, 31–32, 42–45
Maori people: sacred tree of, 58; world tree of, 40
Maple, 14, 97
Marriage, trees and, 78–79
Mastic, Peruvian sacred tree, 59
Maypoles, 81–84

Medicine, trees and, 59, 80, 98–99
Mexico, 93, 98; life tree, 46–48, 52; trees for luck, 78; world tree, 40
Mikamwes, American Indian elf, 72
Mimir, Scandinavian frost-giant, 30
Mulberry, 100–1
Muslims, sacred tree of, 58
Myrtle, Greek sacred tree, 55

Nebuchadnezzar, world tree of, 35–36
New York City, 111–12
New Zealand: sacred tree, 58; world tree, 40
Nidhögg, serpent of Yggdrasil, 30
Nigeria: Amofi tree ceremony, 87–89
Nim tree, oil of, 99
Norns (Fates), 28

Oak, 14, 107–11; Greek "mother tree," 55; life tree, African, 43; life tree, Roman, 43; Russian world tree, 40; sacred, Greek and Roman, 67; sacred groves, Celtic, 56; world tree, Russian, 40
Odin, 30–31, 42–43
Ohio, 94
Oils, 99
Olive oil, 99
Omaha Indians, sacred poles of, 60, 62
Omumborombonga, African life tree, 43
Orange tree, 93
Oxygen from trees, 12, 92

Palestine: trees honoring boys and girls, 78
Palm, 97; date, Egypt, 85
Pan, 67
Peach tree, 96
Pear tree, 97
Pine: Japanese world tree, 36; Switzerland, 84
Planting, 78–79, 106–16; Arbor Day, 114–15; city programs, 111–13; group programs, 111
Poles, 59–64; maypoles, 81–84
Primitive people: beliefs about physical world, 26; trees and, 18–19, 22–24

Pueblo Indians, life tree of, 49, 51
Pygmies, 19–22

Rainmaking, 80
Rain water, 12–13
Ratatösk, squirrel of Yggdrasil, 30
Romans: columns as tree, floral festival, 82; dryads and hamadryads, 66–70; life tree, 43; trees and sons, 78; winter solstice celebrations, 85
Roots, 11, 12–14, 27–28, 30, 31, 32, 35, 37
Runes (stone carvings), 31
Russia: trees and rain, 80; wood demon, 72; wood nymphs, 68; world tree of, 40

Sacred trees, 54–64; Africa, 58–59; Arabia, 58; Asia Minor, 55; Greece, 55–56; groves, Celtic (Druids), 56; India, 57–58; Peru, 59; poles, American Indian, 60–62
San Francisco, Calif., 112–13
Sap, 12, 34–35, 37, 59, 92, 101, 115
Sasabonsum, African wood demon, 73
Sassafras tree, 99
Scandinavia: life tree, 42–43; Wild Huntsman, 74; woodwives in, 71; world tree (Yggdrasil), 27–32, 34, 37, 42
Scotland: fairies in, 70
Seasons and trees, 23, 52, 85–87
Seeds, 18, 23, 35, 55, 92–93, 97, 98, 102, 107, 108
Siberia, 97; world tree of, 37–38
Silk, 100–1
Snakes and world trees, 30, 35, 37
Soma, Hindu world tree, 34–35
Soul, trees and, 45–46, 54, 59
Spirits in trees, 23–24, 58, 59, 65–76, 80–81
Spring, trees and, 86–87
Spruce, 82, 98
Sun pole, 62–64
Switzerland, 94, 115; May Pine trees, 84
Sycamore fig, Egyptian soul tree, 45–46

Talmud, 106–7, 115
Tane-Mahuta, Maori world tree, 40
Tengus, Japanese wood demons, 73
Tibet, 36; world tree, 35
Tigris River, 27, 55
Tooba, sacred tree of Islam, 58
Tota, Aztec world tree, 40
Trees: benefits to man, 12–14, 19, 92–103; characteristics of, 10–12; enjoyment of, 10, 14, 22, 23; uses of, 92–103
Trees of life, see Life trees
Trees, sacred, see Sacred trees
Trees, world, see World trees
Tree worship, see Sacred trees
Trunk, 12, 18, 26, 27, 40

Urd, well of, 28

Virginia, 120

Walnut: love and, 79–80
Wild Huntsman, 71, 73–74, 76
Willow: Czech wood nymph and, 68–70; Japanese life tree, 45; Tibetan world tree, 36
Winter solstice, trees and, 85–86; see also Christmas tree
Women, origin of in trees, 31–32, 42–43
Wood, 81, 92, 101–3
Wood nymphs, see Dryads
Woodwives, 71
World trees, 26–40; Asia Minor, 27; Central Asia, 36–37; China, 36; India, 34–35; Japan, 36; Mexico (Aztecs), 40; Nebuchadnezzar's dream, 35–36; New Zealand, 40; Russia, 40; Scandinavia (Yggdrasil), 27–32, 34, 37, 42; Siberia, 37–38; Tibet, 35

Yakuts, Siberian people, 37–38, 40
Yellow River, 36
Yggdrasil, Scandinavian world tree, 27–32, 34, 37, 42

Zambu, Central Asian world tree, 36–37
Zeus, 43; sacred oak of, 55